Other books in the series:
The Crazy World of Cats (Bill Stott)
The Crazy World of Cricket (Bill Stott)
The Crazy World of Gardening (Bill Stott)
The Crazy World of Golf (Mike Scott)
The Crazy World of the Handyman (Roland Fiddy)
The Crazy World of Hospitals (Bill Stott)
The Crazy World of Jogging (David Pye)
The Crazy World of Love (Roland Fiddy)
The Crazy World of Marriage (Bill Stott)
The Crazy World of Music (Bill Stott)
The Crazy World of the Office (Bill Stott)
The Crazy World of Photography (Bill Stott)
The Crazy World of Rugby (Bill Stott)
The Crazy World of Sailing (Peter Rigby)
The Crazy World of the School (Bill Stott)
The Crazy World of Sex (David Pye)
The Crazy World of Skiing (Craig Peterson & Jerry Emerson)
The Crazy World of Tennis (Peter Rigby)

Published in Great Britain in 1986 by
Exley Publications Ltd, 16 Chalk Hill,
Watford, Herts WD1 4BN, United Kingdom.
Second printing 1990
Third printing 1991

Copyright © Peter Rigby, 1986

ISBN 1-85015-053-2

Printed and bound in Hungary.

the CRAZY world of BIRD WATCHING

Cartoons by
Peter Rigby

EXLEY

"Can you imagine how much time they must spend on preening."

P.J.Rigby.

"I don't know what it is, but whatever you do, don't make a noise like a worm."

"*I've just had a thought Mike. This is no good. The photograph will be upside-down.*"

"*I'm not sure what that was, but put it down as an endangered species.*"

*"Well, of course, they're not going to be fooled if you
don't stand on one leg!"*

"He's been impossible to live with since he sighted a short-toed treecreeper."

"I don't know about you, but when they're in their winter plumage, I'm damned if I can tell the difference."

"That'll be Ferguson. He studied the eating habits of the vulture."

"*Thank goodness they're changing the nest guard. That one's been snoring all night.*"

"Sometimes I think Bradley's never going to master the art of standing on one leg."

"I agree it's not very comfortable, but it really confuses the bird-watchers."

"*Now concentrate everybody, where would you go in winter if you were a Canada goose?*"

"They say this is golden eagle country, but I think we'll be lucky if we spot one."

"For goodness sake will someone tweet or he'll be here all day."

"Just our luck! I thought we may have had a first sighting but it's not even in the book."

"I was just saying, James, that you're very fond of ornithology."

"It's a shame it was your last one. But at least you know it's going to a good home."

P.J.Rigby.

"Then just as they've made a positive identification you make a call like a bald eagle."

"Hear that Karen? If that's not the cry of a bird of prey, I'll eat my hat!"

"Not now – there's bound to be someone watching."

"*I don't know what's the matter with me this morning. It must be that bird-watcher I ate.*"

"I don't think this one's been bird-watching before."

"Is that it, not much of a dawn chorus was it?"

"Binoculars! Binoculars!"

"It's nice to see them in their summer plumage."

"I think she likes you Kevin."

P.J.Rigby.

"*Actually he's not a bird-watcher. He's my wife's private detective.*"

"Fascinating! Now he's ringing her for identification."

"Of course, all this intensive farming makes it hard for the birds to find nesting sites."

"*I'm not complaining. I just think it's insensitive to bring egg sandwiches on a bird-watching trip.*"

"Who's a pretty boy then?"

"I just don't understand it. No one else likes you."

"He's just realised his new equipment didn't include batteries."

P.J.Rigby.

"*Clear off! I've got you down four times already.*"

"1,492, 1,493. . . This people-count gets more difficult every year."

"Listen! There it is again."

"Mavis, did you ever see a film called 'The Birds'?"

"Quiet now, let's see what this one makes of it."

"*Well since you ask. No, I don't think it's kind of cool.*"

"You know, until now, I thought we were the only Bearded Tits around here."

"*In Charles's case, bird-watching is just an excuse to enjoy the freedom of the countryside.*"

P.J.Rigby.

"I must admit to a little help when it comes to spotting them."

"You know that Carrion Crow you're looking for. It just flew off with your lunch."

"Newsdesk?" "I've just spotted the first cuckoo!"

"*Do you think it's some sort of revenge?*"

"*I don't care if you are being immortalized. If you don't come in for your worms now you won't get any.*"

"*It could have been my best work, but this one flew off too.*"

"I see, so he's broken his wing, and she's taking him to the hospital."

"For some peculiar reason they seem to migrate in the summer."

"*Of course, it's not as good as a hide, but it helps.*"

"I suppose it had to happen one day!"

"How disappointing. I thought it was a redwing but it's only superman."

"It'll be even better when we get another pair of binoculars."

"*Your weekend conference bag J.C. Everything's there. Camera, binoculars, bird identification books.*"

"*Doreen, have you been feeding them your cake?*
They're walking home again."

*"What do you mean ruined? This is designer
bird dropping."*

PJ.Rigby.

"I said 'My husband's ignored me since he took up
bird-watching.'"

"*It doesn't hurt much physically. It's just that I never quite saw myself as a thrush's anvil.*"

"For a moment I thought he'd sighted a purple spotted sandpiper, but apparently he's only won the lottery."

"Yuk! I wish you'd wear your glasses Leonard. That's not a lark's nest either."

"I can see now that it's a Boeing 707, but it could have been a rare warbler."

P.J.Rigby.

"Relax. It's just a Common Bearded Friend of the Earth."

"*He's either trapped his finger in the chair or he's imitating the courtship dance of a Titmouse.*"

"If we go very carefully we should spot a skylark on its nest."

"Look Brenda, you'll be glad I had this idea when you see the whimsical bird-studies."

"You thought I was an avocet? I thought you were a bittern."

"It's Mother's Day!"

P.J. Rigby.

"Anyone spotted a skylark yet?"

Books from the "Crazy World" series:

The Crazy World of Cats. £3.99. By Bill Stott. Fat cats, alley cats, lazy cats, sneaky cats – from the common moggie to the pedigree Persian – you'll find them all in this witty collection. If you've ever wondered what your cat was really up to, this is for you.

The Crazy World of Cricket. £3.99. By Bill Stott. This must be Bill Stott's silliest cartoon collection. It makes an affectionate present for any cricketer who can laugh at himself.

The Crazy World of Gardening. £3.99. By Bill Stott. The perfect present for anyone who has ever wrestled with a lawnmower that won't start, over-watered a pot plant or been assaulted by a rose bush from behind.

The Crazy World of Golf. £3.99. By Mike Scott. Over seventy hilarious cartoons show the fanatic golfer in his (or her) every absurdity. What really goes on out on the course, and the golfer's life when not playing are chronicled in loving detail.

The Crazy World of the Handyman. £3.99. By Roland Fiddy. This book is a must for anyone who has ever hung *one* length of wallpaper upside down or drilled through an electric cable. A gift for anyone who has ever tried to "do it yourself" and failed!

The Crazy World of Hospitals. £3.99. By Bill Stott. Hilarious cartoons about life in a hospital. A perfect present for a doctor or a nurse – or a patient who needs a bit of fun.

The Crazy World of Love. £3.99. By Roland Fiddy. This funny yet tender collection covers every aspect of love from its first joys to its dying embers. An ideal gift for lovers of all ages to share with each other.

The Crazy World of Marriage. £3.99. By Bill Stott. The battle of the sexes in close-up from the altar to the grave, in public and in private, in and out of bed. See your friends, your enemies (and possibly yourselves?) as never before!

The Crazy World of Music. £3.99. By Bill Stott. This upbeat collection will delight music-lovers of all ages. From Beethoven to Wagner and from star conductor to the humblest orchestra member, no-one escapes Bill Stott's penetrating pen.

The Crazy World of the Office. £3.99. By Bill Stott. Laugh your way through the office jungle with Bill Stott as he observes the idiosyncrasies of bosses, the deviousness of underlings and the goings-on at the Christmas party.... A must for anyone who has ever worked in an office!

The Crazy World of Photography. £3.99. By Bill Stott. Everyone who owns a camera, be it a Box Brownie or the latest Pentax, will find something to laugh at in this superb collection. The absurdities of the camera freak will delight your whole family.

The Crazy World of Rugby. £3.99. By Bill Stott. From schoolboy to top international player, no-one who plays or watches rugby will escape Bill Stott's merciless exposé of their habits and absurdities. Over seventy hilarious cartoons – a must for addicts.

The Crazy World of Sailing. £3.99. By Peter Rigby. The perfect present for anyone who has ever messed about in boats, gone pea-green in a storm or been stuck in the doldrums.

The Crazy World of the School. £3.99. By Bill Stott. A brilliant and hilarious reminder of those chalk-throwing days. Wince at Bill Stott's wickedly funny new collection of crazy school capers.

The Crazy World of Sex. £3.99. By David Pye. A light-hearted look at the absurdities and weaker moments of human passion – the turn-ons and the turn-offs. Very funny and in (reasonably) good taste.

The Crazy World of Skiing. £3.99. By Craig Peterson and Jerry Emerson. Covering almost every possible (and impossible) experience on the slopes, this is an ideal present for anyone who has ever strapped on skis – and instantly fallen over.

The Crazy World of Tennis. £3.99. By Peter Rigby. Would-be Stephen Edbergs and Steffi Grafs watch out! This brilliant collection will pin-point their pretensions and poses. Whether you play yourself or only watch on TV, this will amuse and entertain you!

These books make super presents. Order them from your local bookseller or from Exley Publications Ltd, Dept BP, 16 Chalk Hill, Watford, Herts WD1 4BN. (Please send £1.50 for one book or £2.25 for two or more to cover postage and packing.)